Cyber Citizenship and Cyber Safety™

The Dangers of Online Predators

Michael Sommers

rosen publishing's
rosen central®

New York

Para Ciber Fo

Published in 2008 by The Rosen Publishing Group, Inc.
29 East 21st Street, New York, NY 10010

First Edition

Library of Congress Cataloging-in-Publication Data

Sommers, Michael A., 1966–
The dangers of online predators / Michael Sommers.—1st ed.
    p. cm.—(Cyber citizenship and cyber safety)
Includes bibliographical references and index.
ISBN-13: 978-1-4042-1350-0 (lib. bdg.)
1. Internet and teenagers. 2. Internet and children. 3. Internet—Safety measures. 4. Online chat groups—Safety measures. 5. Internet abduction—Prevention. I. Title.
HQ799.2.I5S66 2008
004.67'80835—dc22

                                                                2007029521

Manufactured in the United States of America

Contents

Introduction

Alicia was barely thirteen years old when she first met Mac online. At the time, her life resembled that of many teenagers. While she had her run-ins at school with peer pressure and mean kids, she had lots of friends and a happy family life. She also enjoyed spending time surfing the Internet, checking out new Web sites, and instant messaging with friends and people she met online.

When she first chatted with Mac online, she was impressed by his kindness. Over time, they began to IM daily. Each time, the messages were longer, and Alicia began sharing more about her personal life. Gradually, without Alicia noticing, their relationship became more intimate. Mac was very smooth. He never prodded her to share details about her life. Instead,

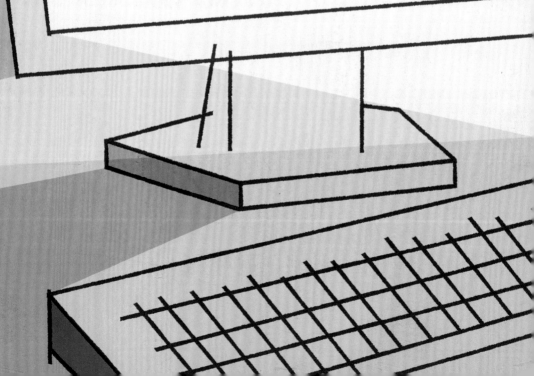

Alicia was convinced that he was interested in her thoughts, feelings, and relationships with friends and family members.

When problems arose at school or home, Alicia was grateful for Mac's advice. She trusted him and was comforted that he was always on her side. Her parents sometimes treated her like a child, but Mac treated her like an adult. He was always online for her. Over time, she began to feel he was the only one who truly understood her. Of course, this was exactly what Mac wanted.

Eventually, Alicia became so dependent on Mac—and isolated from everyone else in her life—that one winter night she found herself walking out of her house, with no coat or money, to meet the person whom she had come to believe was her best friend. The minute she climbed into Mac's car, however, she instinctively knew she had made a terrible mistake.

Mac drove Alicia to his home and wouldn't let her leave. For weeks, he treated her badly and sexually assaulted her. Throughout the horrible period that Alicia was Mac's prisoner, she was determined to survive. She promised herself that when she was rescued, she would devote her life to helping make sure that other teens wouldn't fall victim to the online tactics of such expert and dangerous manipulators.

Miraculously, Alicia was rescued. Having never forgotten her promise, today Alicia is committed to teaching kids how to stay clear of cyber predators. She knows that all kids—no matter what their age, sex, or background—are potential victims.

Katie Tarbox *(above)* fell victim to a sexual predator she first met in an online chat room. The Web site she has since founded is committed to helping other young people stay safe and to supporting victims.

Another young woman, named Katie Tarbox, was also the victim of a cyber predator when she was thirteen. After writing a best-selling book about her terrifying experience, she—like Alicia—wanted to continue to help keep other teens safe. She founded a Web site called Katiesplace.org, which offers safety advice and support to those who have been victims of Internet predators.

Aside from sexual predators, children can be victims of online verbal or emotional abuse by people who use hostile, racist, or sexist language, for example, or who send violent or sexual images. Predators can violate your privacy, contaminate computers with destructive viruses that steal or destroy important files, and even copy and use stolen personal information for illegal activities. Although cyberspace is a fantastic world, people of all ages need to be alert to the fact that there are dangers out there as well. The best way to stay safe is to be aware and educated.

Chapter 1

Generation @

In a very short period of time, the Internet has revolutionized our lives. It has changed the way we buy things, receive our news, listen to music, watch videos and movies, do homework, and socialize.

IRL vs. Online

Your generation—which some people refer to as Generation @—is the first to grow up entirely familiar with the ways of the Web. This is a big advantage since the Internet offers an endless number of resources and information, as well as an essential means of communication that places the entire world at one's fingertips. Yet, along with its many advantages,

Thanks to laptops, cell phones, and wireless Internet connections, young people can be connected to the Web almost anywhere, at any time.

the online world comes with its share of problems and dangers.

There is a big difference between being in cyberspace and IRL (in real life). Although this seems pretty obvious, as an increasing number of people spend more of their lives on the Internet, it's sometimes easy to forget where the boundaries begin and end. Other times, it's hard to remember that what happens online can spill over into real life.

At home and school, you learn about how to act, treat others, and protect yourself in the real world. You may be less aware of them, but similar rules apply in the cyber world. Your parents and teachers might not spend as much time talking about these guidelines (they might not know as much as you do about cyberspace), but this doesn't mean that there aren't correct and incorrect, safe and dangerous ways of behaving when you are online.

It's a Crime

For instance, you know that you are breaking the law when you go into a store and steal a CD. But did you know that downloading music from Web sites without paying for it is illegal? Similarly, just as swearing at or picking on somebody at school can lead to getting kicked out of class, punished, or suspended, writing offensive or aggressive messages to someone online—known as cyber bullying—can get you banned from a Web site or chat room. In the case of violent online threats, the police can even arrest you for harassment.

The tricky thing about the Internet is that many people aren't aware of dangers lurking in cyberspace because they can't see them. In the real world, when you're in a strange neighborhood at night, you're going to be extra careful because you know that you could be in an unsafe situation. However, when it comes to the Internet, you're lured into feeling safe because you're surfing in your own familiar environment. In the real world, you can see a scary-looking thug coming toward you. But in cyberspace, you can't see anybody.

Online thugs are able to enter your computer via e-mail or a pop-up window. They can spread viruses that infect your files or wipe out your hard drive. Similarly, cyber villains can set up fake Web sites that seem legitimate. If they can convince someone into giving out personal information such as a credit card number, they can then charge purchases to that person's bank account.

Cyber Socializing

Blogging, visiting chat rooms, leaving messages on bulletin boards, and creating and surfing profiles on social networking sites are all part of cyber socializing. Increasingly, joining networks such as MySpace or Xanga are becoming a way of life for many young people. These networks allow you to trade messages and information with people who share your interests, anywhere in the world. Some have thousands or even millions of members. As of 2007, for example, MySpace had over forty million members—a population larger than Canada!

For today's Generation @, there is not such a big difference between interacting online and IRL. However, many young people fail to recognize that as they reveal more and more of their personal lives online, they expose themselves to more and more potentially dangerous situations. As cyber socializing has taken off, so have the activities of cyber predators.

Chapter 2

Danger in Cyberspace

Have you ever been in a chat room or online discussion group and had someone say something to you that made you feel uncomfortable? Perhaps the person made a racist, sexist, or prejudiced remark that offended you, or asked a disturbingly personal or even sexual question. He or she might have coaxed you to download images or programs that you suspected your parents wouldn't approve of. Maybe the person even suggested you meet in person to get to know each other or attend a meeting for a group or cause that you'd never heard of or that sounded suspicious.

In North America, it is a crime for an adult to ask anyone under the age of eighteen to take part in any sexual activity. However, it is common. According to recent figures from the National Center for Missing & Exploited Children, one of every five children is sexually solicited over the Internet by predators who try to set up face-to-face meetings with them.

"Don't Talk to Strangers"

Ever since you can remember, you've probably heard adults telling you not to talk to strangers. In our day-to-day life, it's easy to tell who is a stranger and who isn't. After all, the person in question is right in front of you.

On the Internet, however, it's a lot more difficult. How do you know the guy you're talking to in a chat room is really twelve like he says he is? He could be ten or fifteen or thirty-five. In fact, how do you know he's even a guy? He may have e-mailed you a picture of a twelve-year-old that he says is a photo taken of him. But how do you know he didn't copy that photo from another Web site?

One of the great things about the Internet is the number of people we can connect with that we'd never get a chance to meet IRL. The number of contacts and cyber friends we can make is endless. If you've ever checked out some of the personal profiles posted on popular networking sites such as Facebook or Orkut, you'll be amazed by the number of "friends" some young people have.

If you're talking about subjects such as a basketball game, a homemade remedy for zits, or Britney Spears's latest misadventure, there's no problem in how well or not you know your cyber buddy. However, when it comes to giving out personal information, you must be absolutely certain you know with whom you're communicating. And how—unless you've actually met the person face-to-face—can you be sure of anyone?

Just as you would never give your phone number, address, or bank account number to a stranger, you should never think of sharing such precious information with someone in a chat room or on a blog. In the end, there's no way of knowing with whom you're interacting. You might think you're talking to someone your own age or a little older. But in reality, the person could be an adult pretending to be a child so that he or she can gain your trust. He or she could be an online sexual predator.

Posing as a teenage girl, an investigator for the Florida attorney general's Child Predator CyberCrime Unit logs on to a chat room in search of sexual predators.

Portrait of an Online Sexual Predator

When people hear the term "sexual predator," they might imagine a specific type of person. However, there is no one type of adult who sexually exploits, or takes advantage of, children. Sexual predators are more often men, but they can also be women. They can be rich or poor, sixty-six or twenty-six, and can be of any social, ethnic, and religious background. What many people—both kids and their parents—don't imagine is that that nice, supposedly teenage pal you've been IMing with over the last few months is an online predator.

As Internet use has exploded, the dangers to children have dramatically increased. And it doesn't matter where you live. Whether they're after sex or money or something else, predators can safely surf the Net and find names and addresses of other predators and potential victims.

With false screen names and profiles, predators swap child pornography and information in ways that were previously impossible. Offline, sexual predators usually operate by themselves. On the Internet, however, they can share tales of children they've conquered. In chat rooms, they are able to discuss deception techniques and ways to contact children online. They also exchange tips on how to avoid getting caught by the law.

See How They Work

There are different types of online sexual predators. Some will start talking about sexual topics with you right away. Their main interest might be collecting and trading images of child pornography. Your mere presence or your reaction to their comments—whether negative or positive—might excite them. Others might want to meet you face-to-face. They might come right out and say they want to engage in sexual activity with you. Or they may lie and make up another excuse for meeting.

Whether they're after sex or something else, most cyber predators are great manipulators. In fact, the most dangerous ones don't immediately ask you for explicit photos or try to meet with you. Instead, they gradually seduce targets by offering attention, kindness, and even gifts. Often, they'll pretend to be teenagers. They'll listen to you and sympathize with your problems. They'll be aware of the latest music, fashions, expressions, and topics of interest. It's only once you completely trust them that they'll attempt to introduce sexual topics into your conversations.

While some sexual predators only remain online and troll the Internet, others will try to extend their relationship with you into the real world. They might start calling you on the phone. They might send you photos with sexual content and ask you to send them photos of yourself. It is not uncommon for predators to send Polaroid cameras and film as gifts.

By sending you pornographic images of other kids in sexual poses or involved in sexual activities, they'll try to convince you such behavior is normal. They'll take advantage of your natural curiosity and inexperience about sex. At some point, they might even attempt to meet with you or lure you away from home. There are cases of predators who send kids money or bus or plane tickets so they will come visit them.

Who's at Risk

The most common way that online predators contact people is through chat rooms, IM, and e-mail. According to studies carried out by the Crimes Against Children Research Center at the University of New Hampshire in 2001, 20 percent of all kids between ten and seventeen have been sexually solicited over the Internet. Almost 90 percent of these incidents occur either in chat rooms or during IM conversations. If you consider that, in the United States, 25 percent of kids participate in live conversations on computers, and thirteen million use IM, the chances of coming into contact with a predator are high.

Nobody should ever think they are safe from a cyber predator. However, certain types of people seem to be more vulnerable. Most victims tend to be between the ages of eleven and fifteen, and 70 percent are girls. Moreover, loners and risk takers tend to be especially vulnerable to falling into sexual predators' traps.

Loners

Lonely kids who spend a lot of time by themselves are likely victims. Such people might have a troubled family life or feel unpopular at school. Seeking understanding and companionship, they are easily conned by kind strangers they meet online who are sympathetic to their problems and offer them advice and support.

Risk Takers

Kids who like to take chances and live dangerously are also potential victims. Aside from drinking, doing drugs, and engaging in other risky behavior, such kids often want to take chances sexually. Some adolescents are naturally curious about sexuality and

Young teens who feel isolated or unhappy are prime targets for cyber predators, who try to befriend them and gain their trust.

sexual images. They may want to move away from their parents' control and therefore seek new relationships with people outside their home and school. To prove how grown-up they are, they may post seductive photos on their blogs or enter sex or relationship chat rooms in which they pose as older teens and even adults. However, if they encounter a cyber predator, they'll end up with more than they bargained for.

Chapter 3

Troubleshooting: Staying Safe

Surfing and socializing on the Net can be a lot of fun, but like many fun activities, you need to take precautions in order to be safe. For instance, when you play soccer or football, you follow certain rules and wear protective gear so that you won't get hurt. In order to avoid problems in cyberspace, you need to follow rules and take safety precautions, too.

It is scary to think that there are people who use the Internet specifically to victimize kids. Some of them are trying to get your money (or your parents' money). Others may want to influence you and encourage you to get involved in an unhealthy relationship that could involve joining a cult, joining a dangerous or illegal group, or engaging in sex. Following the precautions discussed in this chapter will help ensure that you enjoy the best the Internet has to offer, while staying clear of trouble.

Web Sites

Some Web sites are really interesting and informative, others are full of errors, and still others feature adult material and images that can be inappropriate or even illegal. Adult material refers to pornographic photos and videos. There also may be racist, sexist, and violent content that can be hurtful and that is often illegal. If you come across any such site, don't hang around. Immediately close the window or shut down your browser.

Sometimes, a Web site will ask you to give information about yourself, such as your name, e-mail address, or telephone number, before allowing you to view its contents. You should never give out any personal information without first clearing it with your parents. Personal information includes not only your name, address, phone number, and e-mail address, but also those of your friends or family members.

Whenever you provide information to a Web site or anywhere else in cyberspace, you're giving up some of your privacy. Your information could wind up in a database that can be used to sell you things or send you annoying e-mails. It could also fall into the hands of hackers or predators that want to take advantage of or harm you.

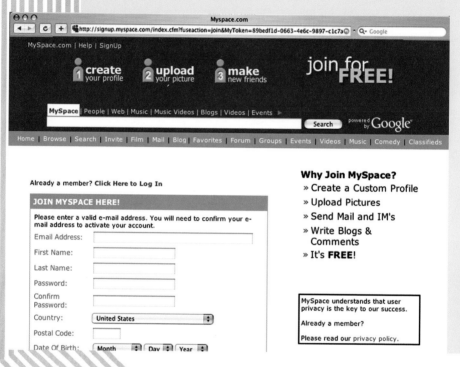

One of the most popular social networking sites is MySpace. No matter what the Web site, remember to look at its privacy policy before providing any personal information.

Remember that even if it seems legitimate, anybody with a bit of training can set up his or her own Web site. This includes perverts, thieves, and criminals. Similarly, if you have your own Web site—or are included on the site of your school, a club, a group, or a team—be careful about what you post on it. Remember that anybody can access such Web sites. For this reason, never include personal information or photos.

Chat Rooms

Chat rooms are great because you can talk about anything under the sun with people all over the world. There are different types of chat rooms. Moderated rooms feature a "speaker" who leads conversations. Other rooms have monitors who can expel people from the rooms if they become rude or abusive. Then there are private, unsupervised rooms, in which it is just you and someone else chatting. These are the rooms that carry the most risk since nobody else can see what goes on.

Chat rooms are where most cyber predators like to strike. Remember that what you type in a chat room can be read by a lot of people, some of whom aren't necessarily who they say they are. For instance, many cyber predators go to teen chat rooms, pretending to be teens themselves. For this reason, no matter how friendly a person seems or how much you think you have in common, always be very careful of what you say. Be suspicious of anyone who tries to get you to do something that you sense is wrong or makes you feel uncomfortable. You should also distrust anyone who criticizes or tries to turn you against your parents, friends, or teachers.

A good tip for staying safe in a chat room is to choose a neutral name that gives away nothing about your identity: something that doesn't include your age or gender, for example. Furthermore, don't use names such as "Kitten" or "Hot Stud,"

Chat rooms are among the most likely places for cyber predators to strike. This is because many people in chat rooms let their guard down since they think of them as "public" places.

which come off as flirty or sexual. They will just attract predators. If you suspect that you are dealing with a potential predator, leave the chat room immediately. Most IM services and chat rooms allow you the option of blocking out people with whom you don't want any contact. By putting a permanent block on a person's name, he or she cannot bother you again.

E-Mail

With a mere mouse click, you can send a message to one or thousands of people via e-mail. Some people and companies send out thousands of e-mails hoping those who receive them will buy products or visit Web sites. This mail is called spam or junk mail.

Although most Internet providers that offer e-mail accounts use protective filters that detect spam, sometimes junk mail might end up in your in-box. Never open an e-mail or attachment if you don't recognize the sender's e-mail address. It could contain messages or links to sites that deal with violent, disturbing, or sexually explicit material. There is also a chance it contains a virus that could infect your entire hard drive and destroy your computer.

Just like the names people use in chat rooms, e-mail addresses can be fake as well. If you receive an e-mail with content that makes you uncomfortable or that is threatening or offensive, report it to your Internet service provider (its address will be on its main Web page). If you think any of the material sent to you is illegal, report it to the CyberTipline at www.cybertipline.com (or call 1-800-843-5768). Illegal content includes threats to your life or safety, or to that of friends or family; pornographic images of children; and any other material related to crimes or criminal activity.

Remember that when you reply to e-mail messages from strangers, you are sending them your e-mail address as well as the name that's on your account. For this reason, it is a good idea not to use your full name. Also be careful what you include in your e-mail messages, even to people you know. Like IM text, both text and photos included in an e-mail can be copied and forwarded to other people without your permission.

Instant Messaging

Instant messaging is a great way to have an online conversation in real time. Instant messages can be exchanged via computers, cell phones, and any other device with Internet access. Messaging is fast and therefore very practical, but it can also be risky. Don't forget that anything you write can be copied and posted anywhere or sent to anybody. Never talk about or send personal information unless you already know the person you're messaging with in real life.

A lot of people IM using a microphone, which allows them to talk with others as if they were having a phone conversation (the bonus is no long-distance charges). Without a phone number, though, you have no way of knowing where the person you're talking to really comes from. With Web cams, you can see the person you're talking to—and they can see you, too. However, did you know that Web cam sessions and audio and video conversations can be easily recorded by the people with whom you're communicating? They can then take these digital images and audio files of you and keep them for themselves, or edit them and post or send them wherever they want.

Cyber predators, in particular, persistently try to get their young victims to take pictures or send videos of themselves, often in sexually suggestive positions. For this reason, you should never exchange photos or Web cam with people you don't know and trust. Similarly, never post or send pictures of friends, family members, or other people without asking their permission. Once these images are in cyberspace, you no longer have control of what happens to them.

Cell phones are a very common way of text messaging and taking and exchanging photos, as well as accessing the Internet.

Peer-to-Peer Services

Peer-to-Peer (P2P) systems allow you to exchange files with other Internet users without the intermediary of a Web site. Services used for swapping music files, for example, are some of the most common. Other P2P systems allow users to share videos, photographs, and software programs. Aside from the fact that file sharing can be illegal (by breaking copyright laws), some downloaded files can have illegal content, such as films or photos of violent or obscene acts, racial or hate crimes, or minors engaged in sexual activity.

P2P sharing systems are potentially problematic because they allow others to gain access to personal material on your computer. This means that complete strangers can download your most personal information and they can also store illegal material on your hard drive. If you do use a file-sharing service, be careful about what "permissions" you give when you set it up. Don't give permission for your own files to be shared. Also refuse offers to install unknown software programs onto your hard drive. Be aware, too, that some P2P systems install spyware or adware programs onto your computer without adequate notice. (Typically the "notice" consists of microtype in a license agreement that is rarely read by users. It's important to read these kinds of agreements very carefully.)

Social Networking Sites

Cyberspace is full of online diaries, personal blogs, photo albums, and social networking sites where people from all over the world post and read profiles that describe their personalities and interests. While expressing yourself can be creative and put you in touch with lots of interesting people, posting too much information can be dangerous. Predators can use this information to find out more about you and then falsely gain your trust.

Myths and Facts

Myth: A person can say or do anything he or she wants online without getting caught.

Fact: Everything online can be traced.

Myth: If you don't give away personal information on the Internet, you can't be found online.

Fact: Predators can piece together information from conversations that you have online in chat rooms or during instant messaging (IM).

Myth: Internet predators are easy to spot.

Fact: In order to create a relationship of trust, most predators initially tend to be very friendly and even charming.

Use good judgment in what you post in a blog, diary, or profile as well as where you post it. Remember that such information is public. All someone has to do is "Google" your name, and he or she can read every intimate detail you care to share.

Going from Online to Real Life

As young people spend increasing amounts of time online, the number of kids who are molested, are kidnapped, or run away from home as a result of getting involved with cyber predators is growing. It is essential to take all the necessary precautio whenever you're engaged in any kind of cyber activity. Also keep in mind that it is one thing to be chatting to a stranger in the safety of your home, from your computer, and quite another to meet someone in the real world.

It doesn't matter how old you are, how long you've known a cyber friend, or how many e-mails, IMs, or even telephone calls you might have exchanged: You should never meet someone offline without taking major precautions. If you do want to meet IRL with someone you've met online, do not go by yourself. Talk to your parents beforehand and have them talk to your cyber friend and his or her parents over the phone. If everything feels OK, arrange to meet in a busy public place like a mall or café. Make sure you bring along one of your parents, and your friend should bring along a parent, too.

It might seem like a big deal to bring a parent with you, but an even bigger deal would be showing up by yourself to meet a person who turns out to be dangerous. Even if you meet in a public place, the person might be armed or could slip a drug in your drink when you're not paying attention. Sound farfetched? Sadly, it isn't.

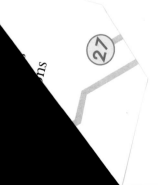

Chapter 4

In the News

In early 1993, a ten-year-old boy was reported missing to the FBI (Federal Bureau of Investigation) after he disappeared from his neighborhood in Brentwood, Maryland. When local police and FBI agents went door-to-door to talk to residents on the boy's street, they encountered two suspicious men who had been befriending boys in the neighborhood. Aside from giving them presents and taking them on vacations, it was discovered that these men had been sexually abusing children for over twenty-five years. More recently, the men had changed their tactics and had set up an online bulletin board service where they shared illegal child pornography photographs. They also used the site to chat with young boys and eventually lure them into face-to-face meetings.

This was the first known U.S. occurrence of sexual predators using the Internet to get to children. At the time, the police and FBI agents were not only shocked by the crimes themselves but also by the fact that sexual predators had started acting online. Investigators arrested the two pedophiles as well as a larger ring of online child pornographers. Tragically, the ten-year-old boy was never found. Meanwhile, when another case came to its attention a year later, the FBI realized this wasn't just an isolated occurrence. It was the beginning of a frightening new trend: sexual exploitation of children over the Internet.

Fighting Cyber Predators

As a consequence, in 1995, the FBI created its Innocent Images National Initiative (IINI). The head office of this special branch of the FBI's Cyber Crimes Program was located in the same Maryland neighborhood where the first terrible cyber crime took place. The IINI has three main goals: To shut down groups of online pedophiles, to stop sexual predators from using the Internet to lure children away from their families, and to rescue child victims

Today, hundreds of full-time agents at more than thirty of the FBI's field offices around the nation participate in undercover IINI operations. In order to find predators, many pretend to be kids or teenagers. They enter chat rooms where predators prowl and wait for them to strike. Sadly, they often don't have to wait long for the predators to take the bait.

FBI supervisory special agent Stacey Bradley of the Innocent Images National Initiative Unit *(above)* monitors possible child pornographers in an online chat room.

By their presence on the Internet, these INII agents succeed in preventing many cyber crimes and protecting a lot of would-be child victims. Since 1995, working with state and local police forces, the IINI has investigated more than 16,000 cases and charged close to 5,000 criminals. However, despite their success and increased efforts and awareness, in recent years, there has been a rise in cases. This is the result of more victims stepping forward to report abuse as well as the increase of young people—and predators—on the Net.

Online Awareness

In a case that occurred in September 2005, a sixteen-year-old girl from Port Washington, New York, fell victim to a cyber predator. The girl met someone on MySpace who claimed he was a teenage boy, and they chatted online a few times.

Although the girl never planned to meet the young man (who actually was thirty-seven), it was easy for him to seek her out in real life. Since she had posted her photo and the name of her after-school job on her profile, all he had to do was show up, uninvited, and wait for the girl to arrive at work. When she did, he followed her to the parking lot, forced her into his car, and attacked her.

This is only one of many examples of how blogging and social networking can lead to serious trouble. It's one thing to list your favorite band or brand of sneakers and quite another to post your phone number, school, job schedule, or other information that makes it easy for anybody with an Internet connection to track you down. According to WiredSafety, an Internet safety group, in the United States alone, each year there are currently around 6,000 reported cases of young people who have fallen victim to cyber predators.

Aside from parents and police, social networks themselves are becoming more concerned about keeping kids safe. Recently, MySpace has tried to enforce a minimum-age requirement of fourteen. It also created special software used to help identify underage users based on information they give. Immediately, the site weeded out over 300,000 profiles. The problem is that many younger teens often lie about their age in their profiles.

Organizations for Kids

Meanwhile, other organizations have been created to help protect kids from—and inform parents and teachers about— cyber crime and abuse. The biggest is WiredSafety (www. wiredsafety.org), a U.S. charity founded in 1995 by Parry Aftab, a cyber lawyer. Aside from helping to prevent and investigate cyber crimes, WiredSafety operates various programs and Web sites that teach safe and responsible Internet use for kids, tweens, teens, and adults. Aside from games, interviews, and articles, kids can report any troubling sites or problems. They can also receive advice from knowledgeable adults and young people who have been victims of cyber predators.

Parry Aftab also started two other groups related to cyber safety. Teenangels (www.teenangels.org) is a group of volunteers between the ages of thirteen and eighteen who have been trained by police and other safety specialists about online safety, privacy, and security. Traveling to schools around the country, they give presentations about how to safely surf the Net. Recently, the group began training Tweenangels, younger volunteers between the ages of nine and twelve. Katiesplace.org, another program of WiredSafety.org, was created by and for young victims of online sexual predators.

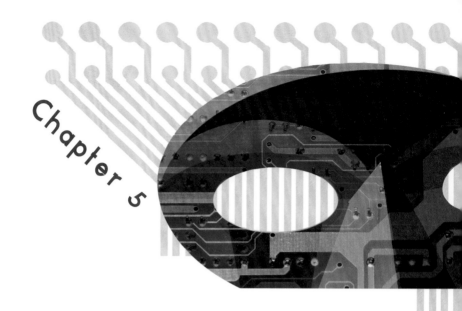

Chapter 5

Resolving Cyber Conflicts

I t's important to know that any kind of sexual harassment or abuse that occurs between an adult and a child—whether it takes place online or offline—is a serious crime. In North America, any adult who persuades or forces a minor to engage in any kind of sexual activity is breaking the law. Sending, receiving, buying, and/or advertising images or material that shows minors in sexual poses or engaging in sexual-related activities (i.e., child pornography) is also against the law.

The Law

Under federal law, it is a serious crime for cyber predators to have children send them sexually provocative photos or videos. It is equally criminal for them to lure children into meeting them offline for the purposes of performing illegal sexual acts. Recently, the U.S. Congress passed new federal laws that increase punishment for adults involved in sexual abuse and child pornography.

Schools and Parents

Almost all public schools in the United States and Canada have Internet access. Consequently, more and more kids are online at school, where they study, do research, and create team, club, or

With computers now in most schools across North America, an increasing number of schools are setting policies that govern students' Internet use.

personal blogs. As computers have become commonplace in schools, teachers and administrators have become more involved in teaching Internet safety. Many schools have adopted agreements that students have to sign before they can log on. Some schools are also creating new rules. One New Jersey private school has banned online social networking for students—even at home and outside of school hours.

Although you spend a lot of time at school, your teachers aren't responsible for you in the same way as your parents are. Ultimately, it's up to you and your parents to work together to make sure you stay safe. In fact, an increasing number of schools let students use the Internet at school only if their parents give their signed consent. Meanwhile, at home, more parents are taking advantage of increasingly sophisticated safety and security systems that limit, control, and monitor cybersurfing.

Secure Software

Many parents—as well as schools and libraries—use filters, blockers, logs, and other security services to protect their children from cyber dangers, including predators. According to a 2005 survey conducted by the Pew Internet & American Life Project, more than half of American families with teenage children use filters to limit access to potentially harmful online content.

Filtering software, such as Cyberpatrol, Safe Eyes, and CYBERsitter, can help control what is seen online. These programs have settings that allow parents to choose certain topics (such as sex, violence, or racism, for example) to be filtered out. This means that when you surf, sites and pages with content that includes certain words or subjects will be off-limits.

Other software allows parents to block access to specific sites, limit the amount of time spent online, or limit the types of communication programs (IM, Web cams) that can be used. Some parents even have monitoring software that will

Although Internet filters and blocks aren't completely foolproof, many parents invest in them since such measures do help ensure safer Internet surfing.

follow every keystroke and register it in a log that they can then check. The newest and most sophisticated of these is called SpectorSoft. Used by police and other law enforcement officials, it keeps track of everything going in and out of a computer.

Although filters and blocks can be useful tools, they are not foolproof. They do end up missing some bad stuff and screening out some good stuff. Moreover, some people have learned how to deactivate or get around filter software. However, despite the limitations, filters and blocks can be useful if used correctly and by taking kids' and parents' concerns into consideration.

The best thing to do is to get a trial download and then spend some time surfing with your parents to see how the filter works for you and the rest of your family. You might not like your parents filtering or blocking what you can and can't access. You might feel like you are being censored or, in the case of monitoring software, that your privacy is being abused. But remember that they are using such software for your safety.

Communication Is Key

It's important for kids and parents to talk about the Internet and how it's used. Your parents should feel that you are protected from things they feel are inappropriate. But you need access to certain types of information for research and projects and to feel that you are not being spied on.

There are many ways of negotiating solutions. For instance, your family could consider using blocking software when your parents aren't around but let you surf unfiltered (if the computer is in a common room like a living room) when they are at home. You might also want to draw up an Internet Usage Agreement (many are available on the sites listed in the back of this book), in which you and your parents agree to certain rules regarding your Internet use.

You may know much more about life online than your parents do. However, your parents have much more life experience than you do. If your parents are overly worried or fearful about things that could happen online, try to reassure them by giving them some online lessons and showing them how amazing the Internet can be. Show them your online profiles and blogs and let them know what Web sites you check out and who your online friends are. Being open and upfront will leave everyone feeling more secure and comfortable. And your parents will probably really appreciate having their cyber-savvy kid explain features of cyberspace to them.

The online world is an amazing place, but so is the offline world. Try to keep a balance between the two. And most important, learn how to surf safely. Laws, rules, filters, and parental monitoring are all there to help protect you from potential dangers. But ultimately, the person who can best defend you from online predators is *you*.

Glossary

blocker Computer software that can be programmed to block a user from accessing certain selected Web sites.

blogging Keeping, writing entries in, or adding material to a web log (blog).

browser Software that lets you find, see, and hear material on the Web, including text, pictures, sound, and video. Popular browsers include Firefox and Microsoft Internet Explorer.

chat rooms Online "rooms" in which users can communicate with each other live, in real time.

cyber bullying Writing offensive or aggressive messages to someone online.

cyberspace The general term used to refer to the electronic areas and communities existing on the Internet, as well as to the culture developing around them.

explicit Portraying nudity or sexual acts in a clear and direct way.

exploitation Unfair treatment or victimization.

filter A software program with settings that allow computer owners to choose certain topics, like sex, violence, or racism, for example, to be placed off-limits when a user is online.

hacker Someone who enters or tries to enter your computer or network without authorization.

harassment The continual bothering, disturbing, or pestering of someone.

intermediary A go-between or negotiator between two sides.

Internet The largest system of linked computers in the world.

IRL An abbreviation for "in real life" (as opposed to online) that is commonly used in chat rooms.

legitimate According to law or recognized rules.

log Monitoring software used by police and other law enforcement officials that keeps track of all information going in and out of a computer.

pedophile An adult who is sexually attracted to children.

pornography Sexually explicit pictures, writing, or other material whose primary purpose is to cause sexual excitement.

posting The sending of a message to a discussion group or other public message area. The message itself is called a post.

predator Someone who preys on people in order to gain something (such as money or sex) from them.

provocative Exciting or stimulating sexual desire.

software A computer program consisting of a set of instructions to be used on your hardware (computer).

solicit To approach a person with an offer of engaging in a sexual activity.

virus A software program capable of reproducing itself that can harm or destroy files or other programs on the same computer.

For More Information

CyberAngels
P.O. Box 3171
Allentown, PA 18106
Web site: http://www.cyberangels.org
   CyberAngels is made up of law enforcement officers, information technology
   specialists, and educators from all over the world who volunteer their time to
   help make the Internet safe for kids and their families through information,
   assistance, and education.

Federal Bureau of Investigation (FBI)
Innocent Images National Initiative
11700 Beltsville Drive, Suite 200
Beltsville, MD 20705-3146
Web site: http://www.fbi.gov/innocent.htm
   The FBI's Innocent Images National Initiative (IINI) teams FBI agents with
   local police around the country, working undercover to investigate online
   predators.

National Center for Missing & Exploited Children (NCMEC)
Charles B. Wang International Children's Building
699 Prince Street
Alexandria, VA 22314-3175
(703) 274-3900
Hotline: (800) THE-LOST (843-5678)
Web site: http://www.missingkids.com
   In addition to helping prevent child abduction and sexual exploitation,
   NCMEC offers a "CyberTipline" for reporting possible illegal Internet
   activity related to child pornography, predation, or other types of child
   sexual exploitation.

NetSmartz Workshop
Charles B. Wang International Children's Building
699 Prince Street
Alexandria, VA 22314-3175
(800) THE-LOST (843-5678)
Web site: http://www.netsmartz.org
NetSmartz is an educational safety resource from the National Center for Missing & Exploited Children and Boys & Girls Clubs of America for children, teens, parents, teachers, and law enforcement.

Public Safety Canada
269 Laurier Avenue West
Ottawa, ON K1A 0P8
Canada
(800) 622-6232
Web site: http://www.safecanada.ca
This government of Canada Web site offers information and links to services on all topics related to safety of its citizens.

Web Sites

Due to the changing nature of Internet links, Rosen Publishing has developed an online list of Web sites related to the subject of this book. This site is updated regularly. Please use this link to access the list:

http://www.rosenlinks.com/cccs/onpr

For Further Reading

Appleman, Dan. *Always Use Protection: A Teen's Guide to Safe Computing*. Berkeley, CA: Apress, 2004.

Farnham, Kevin, and Dale Farnham. *MySpace Safety: 51 Tips for Teens and Parents*. Pomfret, CT: How-to Primers, 2006.

Rothman, Kevin F. *Coping with Dangers on the Internet: A Teen's Guide to Staying Safe Online*. New York, NY: Rosen Publishing Group, 2000.

Schwartau, Winn. *Internet and Computer Ethics for Kids (and Parents & Teachers Who Haven't a Clue)*. Seminole, FL: Interpact Press, 2001.

Tarbox, Katie. *A Girl's Life Online: My Story*. New York, NY: Plume, 2004.

Vos MacDonald, Joan. *Cybersafety: Surfing Safely Online* (Teen Issues). Berkeley Heights, NJ: Enslow Publishers, Inc., 2001.

Bibliography

CBS News. *The Early Show.* "Key to Protecting Kids Online? Talk!" CBSNews.com. April 5, 2006. Retrieved June 2007 (http://www.cbsnews.com/stories/2006/04/05/earlyshow/living/parenting/main1473951.shtml).

CyberAngels. Retrieved June 2007 (http://www.cyberangels.org).

Enough Is Enough: Making the Internet Safer for Children and Families. Statistics. Retrieved June 2007 (http://enough.org/inside.php?id=2UXKJWRY8#6).

Federal Bureau of Investigation. Innocent Images National Initiative. Retrieved June 2007 (http://www.fbi.gov/innocent.htm).

Frum, Larry, Jr. "Are Your Teens Safe Online?" WFTV.com. November 22, 2006. Retrieved June 2007 (http://www.wftv.com/family/10347056/detail.html).

Hansen, Chris. "Dangers Children Face Online." *Dateline.* MSNBC.com. November 11, 2004. Retrieved June 2007 (http://www.msnbc.msn.com/id/6083442).

Hempel, Jessi. "Protecting Your Kids from Cyber-Predators." *Business Week.* December 12, 2005. Retrieved June 2007 (http://www.businessweek.com/magazine/content/05_50/b3963015.htm).

Hughes, Donna Rice. "Sexual Predators Online." ProtectKids.com. 2001. Retrieved June 2007 (http://www.protectkids.com/dangers/onlinepred.htm).

Katiesplace.org. Retrieved June 2007 (http://www.
Katiesplace.org).

Mihelich, Peggy. "Protect Your Children from Online
Predators." CNN.com. March 23, 2007. Retrieved June
2007 (http://www.cnn.com/2007/TECH/internet/
03/23/safeonline.101/index.html).

NetSmartz Workshop. Retrieved June 2007 (http://www.
netsmartz.org).

Regnier, Pat. "Keep Your Kids Safe." *Money*. December 7, 2006.
Retrieved June 2007 (http://money.cnn.com/2006/
12/05/magazines/moneymag/cybersafety_kids.
moneymag/index.htm).

Safekids.com. Retrieved June 2007 (http://www.
safekids.com).

Safe Surfing! A Kid's Guide to Etiquette on the Net.
Retrieved June 2007 (http://www.safekids.com).

WiredSafety.org. Retrieved June 2007 (http://www.
wiredsafety.org).

Index

About the Author

Michael A. Sommers was born in Texas and raised in Canada. After earning a bachelor's degree in English literature at McGill University in Montreal, Canada, he went on to complete a master's degree in history and civilizations from the École des Hautes Études en Sciences Sociales in Paris, France. For the last fifteen years, he has worked as a writer and photographer and has written various books for Rosen, including *Everything You Need to Know About Safe Internet Romance*, which won a 2002 VOYA award.

Photo Credits

Cover Les Kanturek; p. 6 © Amy Etra/Time & Life Pictures/Getty Images; p. 8 © www.istockphoto.com/lewis long; pp. 13, 22, 31 © AP Image; p. 17 © www.istockphoto.com/Bobbie Osborne; p. 25 © Steve Smith/Photographer's Choice/Getty Images; p. 35 © Henning von Holleben/Photonica/Getty Images.

Photo Researcher: Amy Feinberg